OCCASIONS

Other Poetry Collections Edited by Anne Harvey

In Time of War

Something I Remember

A Picnic of Poetry

The Language of Love

OCCASIONS
every day and special day happenings

Poems selected by Anne Harvey

Illustrated by Angela McAllister

Blackie

Blackie and Son Ltd
7 Leicester Place
London WC2H 7BP

Printed in Great Britain

Contents

Introduction 7

This Day Dawning 9

The Child's Calendar 19

Birthdays 67

No School Today 81

Forget Not This Day 111

Index of First Lines 154

Acknowledgements 158

for my brother and sisters
John, Jeanne and Carolyn
and for 'the Mills girls next door'
remembering Totteridge Fields
and many occasions

'We'll talk of sunshine and of song,
And Summer days when we were young;
Sweet childish days that were as long
    As twenty days are now.'

WILLIAM WORDSWORTH

Introduction

When I first started collecting poems for this book people asked, 'What exactly do you mean by an occasion?' My immediate answer was 'Almost anything that happens'. It soon became clear to me that it was not the big, important events that really made the most interesting poetry. State occasions, royal and historical events, wars and politics . . . these were best left to the history books. It seemed to be the small happenings that poets could bring to life for us.

Each of our lives is filled with occasions from the important moment of our birth — the first of all occasions — onwards. If, for example, I take yesterday, an ordinary February Sunday, here are some of the occasions I experienced:

1) Breakfast in bed (lazy thing, I can hear you say). I'm not usually so spoilt but was working very late the night before!

2) A walk in Kew Gardens where the daffodils and crocuses were glorious and the magnolia trees' flowers were opening waxy petals. Everything unexpectedly early this year. (See two poems about Kew Gardens on pages 41 and 42.)

3) A surprise visit from Edwin who lives next door but one, bringing me a thank-you bunch of yellow tulips, because I'd helped him with a poem for school.

4) Some time spent with ten-month-old Thomas, next door. He seems to change and grow each day, and yesterday he was full of smiles, because he'd just learnt to crawl and his first tooth was through.

5) The day ended in a very restless night with strong gales sweeping the countryside again this year. Part of our garden fence was shattered, the crocuses on the window-sill blown to purple fragments. The daffodils survived, but all over the country there were disasters.

Not a very exciting day you might think, but a poet's skill and imagination could turn any one of these happenings into a poem.

Each anthology I make becomes a landmark for me. This one feels like a real *occasion*.

Anne Harvey
February 1990

This

Day

Dawning

A short section but the poems make big statements about the importance of each single day. Each day is there for us to snatch at; deserves to be lived to the full. The poet John Dryden, writing in the 17th Century, said:

> Happy the man, and happy he alone,
> He who can call today his own:
> He who, secure within, can say,
> Tomorrow do thy worst, for I have lived today.

Someone wrote that in my autograph book when I was ten, and now I know what it means.

Robert Browning, in the 19th Century, wrote a drama called *Pippa Passes* about a little Victorian girl who had only one day's holiday a year from her factory job. She treasured that day, knew she must not waste a precious second of her 'twelve hours treasure'.

Imagine her excitement . . .

> What shall I please today?
> My morn, noon, eve, and night, — how spend my day?
> Tomorrow I must be Pippa who winds silk,
> The whole year round to earn just bread and milk:
> But this one day, I have leave to go,
> And play out my fancy's fullest games . . .

I think Pippa would approve of the way the following poets lived their days. Not all days are so perfect.

Pippa's Song

> The year's at the Spring
> And day's at the morn;
> Morning's at seven;
> The hill-side's dew-pearled;
> The lark's on the wing;
> The snail's on the thorn;
> God's in His Heaven—
> All's right with the world!

ROBERT BROWNING

Sunrise

Look to this day!
For it is life, the very life of life.
In its brief course
Lie all the verities and realities of your existence:
    The bliss of growth
    The glory of action
    The splendour of achievement,
For yesterday is but a dream
And tomorrow is only a vision,
But today well lived makes every yesterday
    a dream of happiness
And tomorrow a vision of hope.
Look well, therefore, to this day!
Such is the salutation to the dawn.

FROM THE SANSKRIT

O I Have Dined on This Delicious Day

O I have dined on this delicious day,
on green-salad treetops wet with beaded
water, tossed by the fork tines of the wind;
devoured the crouton water-birds and
every crumb and crust of the dark-bread earth;
through gristle to the marrowbone of rocks
and the wrinkled grain of high-loaf hills — all
garnished by kindled bush and windrow grass.

O I have bitten into this bright day
and drunk from the clean basin of its sky
till only the clouds were left clinging to
my glass and the sun turned on its spit
into grape-press night and finished with
a frosted melon-ball of yellow moon.

RICHARD SNYDER

'I am Cherry Alive' The Little Girl Sang

'I am cherry alive,' the little girl sang,
'Each morning I am something new.
I am apple, I am plum, I am just as excited
As the boys who made the Hallowe'en bang;
I am tree, I am cat, I am blossom too:
When I like, if I like, I can be something new,
Someone very old, a witch in a zoo:

I can be someone else whenever I think who,
And I want to be everything sometimes too:
And the peach has a pit and I know that too,
And I put it in along with everything
To make the grown-ups laugh whenever I sing:
And I sing: *It Is True, It Is Untrue;*
I know, I know, the true is untrue,
The peach has a pit, the pit has a peach:
And both may be wrong
When I sing my song,
But I don't tell the grown-ups: because it is sad,
And I want them to laugh just like I do
Because they grew up
And forgot what they knew
And they are sure
I will forget it one day too.
They are wrong. They are wrong.
Then I sang my song, I knew, I knew!
I am red,
I am gold,
I am green,
I am blue.
I will always be me,
I will always be new!'

DELMORE SCHWARZ

Greetings

'Good morning, my husband,' I said,
'Where have you been and what have you seen,
What's new?'

'Hmmm?' said her husband, 'Hmmm?'

'Good morning, my sons,' I said,
'Where have you been and what have you seen?
What's new?'

'Excuse us, please,' said sons,
'We've things to do.'

'Good morning, my dog,' I said,
'Where have you been and what have you seen,
What's new?'

'Why, everything's new,' said dog,
'The sun that bounced into the sky
Is quite a different sun
To the one that rolled behind the hills
Last night, just as darkness fell;
And the grass is full of brand-new scents,
Most marvellous and interesting;
And birds are singing different songs —
Oh, everything's new,' said dog.

'Good morning, my cat,' I said,
'Where have you been and what have you seen?
What's new?'

But cat only narrowed his golden eyes
And asked if his milk was there.

ANNE BELL

Good Times

My daddy has paid the rent
and the insurance man is gone
and the lights is back on
and my uncle Brud has hit
for one dollar straight
and they is good times
good times
good times

My Mama has made bread
and Grampaw has come
and everybody is drunk
and dancing in the kitchen
and singing in the kitchen
oh these is good times
good times
good times

Oh children think about the
good times

LOUISE CLIFTON

This Day Dawning

This day dawning is the black fruitgum,
the sixpence in the pudding; the day
Dad first let go the bicycle's saddle.
It is my mother's knee, the ease
when the toothache had gone.

It is the day I was appointed —
and the day I was released.
It is every bill in the house paid off.
This day is cyclamen and holly
dancing to a daffodil band.

It is the day when Olive said *yes*.
Bubbles in a baby's bath, balloons
and his first bouncing words.
It is the day my son returned home;
my daughter singing in the choir.

It is the Christmas stockings filled;
the tightly rolled-up fiver
in the Salvation Army tin.
Top hat and tails and taxis
and that first successful waltz.

It is Pickering Park and Costello;
one magnificent minnow
in a jam jar bright with rainbows.
It is the uncashed cheque for one guinea
for a first ever poem in print.

This day dawning is the taste returning
after a bout of heavy cold.
It is the irresistible invitation
of a vast untrodden snow
and only I can put my foot in it.

MAURICE RUTHERFORD

*I'm someone who always goes for the black fruitgums so the first line of
that poem appealed to me. It's the sort of poem that can give you ideas
about the events that make you feel good. I might have written —*

> It is the day I gave up teaching,
> The day I first wore green,
> The first play I ever saw . . .

Tomorrows

Tomorrows never seem to stay,
Tomorrows will be yesterday
Before you know.
Tomorrows have a sorry way
Of turning into just today,
And so . . . and so . . .

DAVID McCORD

The

Child's

Calendar

Poets seem to write more about the four seasons than any other subject, and most of us write our very first poem about Spring. I did. And I was extremely proud of it, with its rhymes of 'spring and wing', 'green and seen', 'flower and shower'. In those days we always made our poems rhyme at school. I didn't realise how unoriginal my poem was, all about leaves and buds, and bird-song, and flowers shooting up. Nowadays I look for a fresher treatment of a well-known theme. In L A G Strong's poem on page 31 we know it's Spring because 'Old Dan'l's out again', and Barbara Euphan Todd in her poem on page 65 knew that Spring had come, not by the usual signs, but,

> Because there were whips and tops
> By the jars of lollipops
> In the two little village shops.

The seasons have changed over the years too. That old favourite 'The Months' (not in this book, but in many others) starts with

> January brings the snow
> Makes our feet and fingers glow . . .

which isn't always true.

You'll find some weather poems here, but also others where poets offer a very individual response to the days of the year. Perhaps a certain event made a big impression, or triggered a memory.

Easter in Hawaii, and Christmas in the Caribbean make a change from the familiar; firework night ends in tears here and summer's end is marked by 'a pair of worn-out tennis shoes'.

George Mackay Brown lives in the Orkney Islands where he was born and his writing is very firmly rooted in its traditions, climate and countryside. His calendar is unusual; I marvel at the way it only takes him nine words to highlight the invasion of holiday-makers in July.

A Child's Calendar

No visitors in January.
A snowman smokes a cold pipe in the yard.

They stand about like ancient women,
The February hills.
They have seen many a coming and going, the hills.

In March, Moorfea is littered
With knock-kneed lambs.

Daffodils at the door in April,
Three shawled Marys.
A lark splurges in galilees of sky.

And in May
A russet stallion shoulders the hill apart.
The mares tremble.

The June bee
Bumps in the pane with a heavy bag of plunder.

Strangers swarm in July
With cameras, binoculars, bird books.

He thumped the crag in August,
A blind blue whale.

September crofts get wrecked in blond surges.
They struggle, the harvesters.
They drag loaf and ale-kirn into winter.

In October the fishmonger
Argues, pleads, threatens at the shore.

Nothing in November
But tinkers at the door, keening, with cans.

Some December midnight
Christ, lord, lie warm in our byre.
Here are stars, an ox, poverty enough.

GEORGE MACKAY BROWN

Good Riddance But Now What?

Come children, gather round my knee;
Something is about to be.

Tonight's December thirty-first,
Something is about to burst.

The clock is crouching, dark and small,
Like a time bomb in the hall.

Hark! It's midnight, children dear.
Duck! Here comes another year.

OGDEN NASH

The New Year

He was the one man I met up in the woods
That stormy New Year's morning; and at first sight,
Fifty yards off, I could not tell how much
Of the strange tripod was a man. His body
Bowed horizontal, was supported equally
By legs at one end, by a rake at the other:
Thus he rested, far less like a man than
His wheel-barrow in profile was like a pig.
But when I saw it was an old man bent,
At the same moment came into my mind
The games at which boys bend thus, *High-cocolorum,*
Or *Fly-the-garter,* and *Leap-frog;* At the sound
Of footsteps he began to straighten himself;
His head rolled under his cape like a tortoise's;
He took an unlit pipe out of his mouth
Politely ere I wished him 'A Happy New Year',
And with his head cast upward sideways muttered —
So far as I could hear through the trees' roar —
'Happy New Year, and may it come fastish, too,'
While I strode by and he turned to raking leaves.

EDWARD THOMAS

*If you read that poem again — and perhaps again — the pictures will be
very sharp. The man bent over like a camera-stand or tripod; his wheel-
barrow sideways on looking like a pig. Edward Thomas, who was
killed in the First World War in France, had a keen observant eye.
Friends who walked with him said there was nothing he missed.*

January 20th

St Agnes' Eve — Ah, bitter chill it was!
The owl, for all his feathers, was a-cold;
The hare limp'd trembling through the frozen grass,
And silent was the flock in woolly fold:

JOHN KEATS

Ode to a Sneeze

I sneezed a sneeze into the air,
It fell to earth I know not where,
But hard and froze were the looks of those
In whose vicinity I snooze.

ANON

Kit Wright (Britain's tallest poet) set this next poem in Canada. It's a really happy, sparky poem. He calls it a 'stomp' because of the strong rhythm, and talks of the 'filmic effect' of the red boots against the white snow.

Red Boots On

Way down Geneva,
All along Vine,
Deeper than the snow drift
Love's eyes shine:

Mary Lou's walking
In the winter time.

She's got

Red boots on, she's got
Red boots on,
Kicking up the winter
Till the winter's gone.

So

Go by Ontario,
Look down Main,
If you can't find Mary Lou,
Come back again:

Sweet light burning
In winter's flame.

She's got

Snow in her eyes, got
A tingle in her toes
And new red boots on
Wherever she goes

So

All around Lake Street,
Up by St Paul,
Quicker than the white wind
Love takes all:

Mary Lou's walking
In the big snow fall.

She's got

Red boots on, she's got
Red boots on,
Kicking up the winter
Till the winter's gone.

KIT WRIGHT

There Goes Winter

Look at red-faced Winter
Come slouching down the road,
Coughing and puffing
In his tatty grey overcoat and scarf,
Dew-drop on the end of his nose!

Watch his frosty breath
Turn the rain white and fragile,
Stiffen pond and puddle,
Make ground tight-fisted,
Spike the eaves with icicles!

Listen how he brings
Shivers and shudders,
Grumbles and groans
To pavements, roadways,
Car-parks and playgrounds!

Old dawdler! —
But wait, watch him shuffle
Over that hill
Into a green dream
Of snowdrop, crocus coming our way!

MATT SIMPSON

Eleanor Farjeon was born on February 13th 1881 and wished it had been the 14th, Valentine's Day, so that her parents would have called her Valentine. She was always very romantic, and wrote this poem when she was only seven, in 1888, to her sweetheart, Button.

Keep True to Me: A Valentine

My heart has never beat before,
As it did beat just now;
I want you but to keep to me
And I'll give my hand to thou.

I'll *never* turn away from thee,
If always you keep true;
But if you always turn away,
I will not keep to you.

But I will go out far away,
And find a lover true to me;
But if you never turn away,
I'll never, never turn from thee.

You've turned away from me just once,
But if you won't again;
I'll give you all the love my heart,
Will ever and can contain.

ELEANOR FARJEON

March

Dear March — Come in —
How glad I am —
I hoped for you before —
Put down your Hat —
You must have walked —
How out of Breath you are —
Dear March, how are you, and the Rest —
Did you leave Nature well —
Oh March, Come right up stairs with me —
I have so much to tell —

I got your Letter, and the Birds —
The Maples never knew that you were coming — till I
called
I declare — how Red their Faces grew —
But March, forgive me — and
All those Hills you left for me to Hue —
There was no Purple suitable —
You took it all with you —

Who knocks? That April.
Lock the Door —
I will not be pursued —
He stayed away a Year to call
When I am occupied —
But trifles look so trivial
As soon as you have come

That Blame is just as dear as Praise
And Praise as mere as Blame —

EMILY DICKINSON

*Rather like the modern poet, Matt Simpson, in 'There Goes Winter'
(page 28) the Victorian poet, Emily Dickinson, sees the month as a
person arriving after a long walk. 'How out of breath you are' is a clever
way of suggesting March is windy.*

Old Dan'l

Out of his cottage to the sun
Bent double comes old Dan'l,
His chest all over cotton wool,
His back all over flannel.

'Winter will finish him,' they've said
Each winter now for ten:
But come the first warm day of Spring
Old Dan'l's out again.

L A G STRONG

To my Sister

It is the first mild day of March:
Each minute sweeter than before,
The redbreast sings from the tall larch
That stands beside our door.

There is a blessing in the air,
Which seems a sense of joy to yield
To the bare trees, and mountains bare,
And grass in the green field.

My sister! ('tis a wish of mine)
Now that our morning meal is done,
Make haste, your morning task resign;
Come forth and feel the sun.

Edward will come with you – and pray,
Put on with speed your woodland dress;
And bring no book: for this one day
We'll give to idleness.

WILLIAM WORDSWORTH

William Wordsworth lived much of his life in the Lake District and his sister Dorothy was often his close companion. Sometimes an entry in her diary gave him the idea for a poem.

Good-by My Winter Suit

Good-by my winter suit,
good-by my hat and boot,
good-by my ear-protecting muffs
and storms that hail and hoot.

Farewell to snow and sleet,
farewell to cream of wheat,
farewell to ice-removing salt
and slush around my feet.

Right on! to daffodils,
right on! to whippoorwills,
right on! to chirp-producing eggs
and baby birds and quills.

The day is on the wing,
the kite is on the string,
the sun is where the sun should be —
it's spring all right! It's Spring!

N M BODECKER

A whippoorwill is a North American bird, rather like a night-jar. Its song can be very noisy, and keep you awake at night.

I've known this next poem for over twenty years, and enjoy its confident, light-hearted play on words.

April

So here we are in April, in showy, blowy April,
　　In frowsy, blowsy April, the rowdy, dowdy time;
In soppy, sloppy April, in wheezy, breezy April,
　　In ringing, stinging April, with a singing swinging
　　　　rhyme!

The smiling sun of April on the violets is focal,
　　The sudden showers of April seek the dandelions out;
The tender airs of April make the local yokel vocal,
　　And he raises rustic ditties with a most melodious
　　　　shout.

So here we are in April, in tipsy gypsy April,
　　In showery, flowery April, the twinkly, sprinkly days;
In tingly, jingly April, in highly wily April,
　　In mighty, flighty April with its highty-fighty ways!

The duck is fond of April, and the clucking chickabiddy
　　And other barnyard creatures have a try at carolling;
There's something in the air to turn a stiddy kiddy giddy,
　　And even I am forced to raise my croaking voice and
　　　　sing.

TED ROBINSON

The first of April, some do say
Is set apart for All Fools' Day,
But why the people call it so,
Nor I nor they themselves do know.

RHYME IN 'Poor Robin's Almanack 1760'

Every year I played the same April Fool trick on my poor father. I'd
rush down to breakfast, gobble up my boiled egg, turn the empty shell
upside down and place it in his egg-cup. He would solemnly, annually,
crack the shell open, and be immensely amazed at the hollowness inside.
    The boy in Richard Edwards' poem is far more inventive!

A Day in Spring

I was lying in the bath
With the squidgy soap at hand
When a shout came from the garden:
'It's coming in to land!
It's saucer-shaped, it's huge,
It's come from outer space!
There's something at the porthole:
A hand? A foot? A face!
It's gliding past the roof,
It's hovering silently,
And now the hatch is opening . . .
Whatever can *that* be?

Six arms, four legs, a tail,
A head shaped like a bell,
It's floating down towards me,
Oh, no!' . . . then silence fell.

I slithered through the suds,
I splashed out of the tub,
I wrapped a towel around me,
No time for rub-a-dub,
I hurried to the window,
I clambered on a stool,
I looked down at . . . my brother
Grinning upwards: 'April Fool!'

RICHARD EDWARDS

This Easter poem is filled with sound of birds, bees, bells and brook, and also shows a very private way of celebrating Easter.

Easter Morning

Laden with bud and unfolding leaf
The hedge is alive with sound.
Chaffinch, sparrow and blue tit challenge rivals,
Scold my presence here.
Droning bees quarter from flower to flower,
Daisy, celandine and primrose.
In silence a shy dunnock creeps among rockery stones.
The persistent clicking of starlings
And the 'jack jack' of a daw
Penetrate the crescendo of blackbird aria.
A wren swollen with song claims the dry stone wall.

The sun climbs higher.
Vigorous quarrels in the hedge subside.
A church bell tongues softly,
Invites worshippers into cool dimness of prayer.
But here, where a stream bubbles laughter
Over its boulder bed,
Here in soft sunshine
Is my church,
Here in this garden.

CATHERINE BENSON

From Easter: Wahiawa, 1959

The rain stopped for one afternoon.
Father brought out
his movie camera and for a few hours
we were all together
under a thin film
that separated the rain showers
from that part of the earth
like a hammock
held loosely by clothespins.

Grandmother took the opportunity
to hang the laundry
and Mother and my aunts
filed out of the house
in pedal pushers and poodle cuts,
carrying the blue washed eggs.

Grandfather kept the children
penned in on the porch,
clucking at us in his broken English
whenever we tried to peek
around him. There were bread crumbs
stuck to his blue gray whiskers.

I looked from him to the sky,
a membrane of egg whites
straining under the weight
of the storm that threatened
to break.

We burst loose from Grandfather
when the mothers returned
from planting the eggs
around the soggy yard.
He followed us,
walking with stiff but sturdy legs.
We dashed and disappeared
into bushes,
searching for the treasures;
the hard-boiled eggs
which Grandmother had been simmering
in vinegar and blue colour all morning.

CATHY SONG

Cathy Song was born in Honolulu, Hawaii in 1955. That's a long way from the North London suburb of my childhood, but we, too, hard-boiled our eggs in red, blue and green colouring at Easter, dying our mother's saucepans . . .

Kew in Lilac-Time

Go down to Kew in lilac-time, in lilac-time, in lilac-time;
Go down to Kew in lilac-time (it isn't far from London!)
And you shall wander hand-in-hand with love in
    summer's wonderland;
Go down to Kew in lilac-time (it isn't far from London!).

The cherry trees are seas of bloom and soft perfume
    and sweet perfume,
The cherry trees are seas of bloom (and oh! so near to
    London!)
And there they say, when dawn is high, and all the
    world's a blaze of sky,
The cuckoo, though he's very shy, will sing a song for
    London.

The nightingale is rather rare and yet they say
    you'll hear him there
At Kew, at Kew, in lilac-time (and oh! so near to
    London!)
The linnet and the throstle, too, and after
    dark the long halloo
And golden-eyed *tu-whit, tu-whoo* of owls that ogle
    London.

For Noah hardly knew a bird of any kind that isn't heard
At Kew, at Kew, in lilac-time (and oh! so near to
    London!)
And when the rose begins to pout, and all the
    chestnut spires are out,
You'll hear the rest without a doubt, all chorusing for
    London:

Come down to Kew in lilac-time, in lilac-time, in lilac-time,
Come down to Kew in lilac-time (it isn't far from London!)
And you shall wander hand-in-hand with love in
    summer's wonderland;
Come down to Kew in lilac-time (it isn't far from London!).

ALFRED NOYES

'Come down to Kew —'

You know, of course, that pleasant rhyme,
'Come down to Kew in Lilac-time':
I often feel it isn't fair
To other flowers growing there;
So I intend to write a rhyme,
'Come down to Kew at *any* time.'

Come down to Kew, I mean to say,
When Bluebells paint the woods of May;
Come down to Kew, shall be my tune,
When Roses, rioting in June,
Usher the summer pageant in
Until the Autumn days begin.

Come down to Kew; though days are cold,
The leaves are yellow, brown and gold.
Come down to Kew, I mean to write,
And see the Winter Aconite;
Its little ruff is wet with rime —
Come down to Kew at any time.

REGINALD ARKELL

All in June

A week ago I had a fire,
 To warm my feet, my hands and face;
Cold winds, that never make a friend,
 Crept in and out of every place.

Today, the fields are rich in grass,
 And buttercups in thousands grow;
I'll show the World where I have been —
 With gold-dust seen on either shoe.

Till to my garden back I come,
 Where bumble-bees, for hours and hours,
Sit on their soft, fat, velvet bums,
 To wriggle out of hollow flowers.

W H DAVIES

For some of his life W H Davies lived the life of a tramp in England and America.

Summer Evening

The sandy cat by the Farmer's chair
Mews at his knee for dainty fare;
Old Rover in his moss-greened house
Mumbles a bone, and barks at a mouse.
In the dewy fields the cattle lie
Chewing the cud 'neath a fading sky;
Dobbin at manger pulls his hay:
Gone is another summer's day.

WALTER DE LA MARE

End of Summer Term

Tonight, tonight, the pillow fight,
Tomorrow's the end of school,
Break the dishes, break the chairs,
Trip the teachers on the stairs.

Four more days and we are free
From the school of misery.
No more pencils, no more books,
No more teachers' grumpy looks!

ANON

August

And is this August weather? Nay,
    not so.
  With the long rain the cornfield
    waxeth dark.
  How the cold rain comes pouring
    down! and hark
To the chill wind whose measured
    pace and slow
Seems still to linger, being loth to go.
  I cannot stand beside the sea and
    mark
  Its grandeur — it's too wet for that:
    no lark
In this drear season cares to sing or
    show.
And, since its name is August, all
    men find
  Fire not allowable; winter foregone
    Had more of sunlight and of
    glad warmth more.
    I shall be fain to run upon the
    shore
  And mark the rain. Hath the
    sun ever shone?
Cheer up! there can be nothing
    worse to mind.

CHRISTINA ROSSETTI

The End-of-Summer Tennis Shoes Blues

The tread is gone
from both the soles,
And both the toes
are full of holes.

But that is not
the worst of it —
My tennis shoes
no longer fit!

Sing the end-of-summer blues,
Good-bye, my old tennis shoes.

JUDITH UNTER

Autumn Morning at Cambridge

I ran out in the morning, when the air was clean and new
And all the grass was glittering and grey with autumn
   dew,
I ran out to an apple-tree and pulled an apple down,
And all the bells were ringing in the old grey town.

Down in the town off the bridges and the grass,
They are sweeping up the leaves to let the people pass,
Sweeping up the old leaves, golden-reds and browns,
Whilst the men go to lecture with the wind in their
gowns.

FRANCES CORNFORD

Frances Cornford was the grand-daughter of the famous naturalist
Charles Darwin. She lived all her life in Cambridge and knew every
corner of it.

Poem for the Changing of the Clocks

This hour
  in the night
    When I wait
      in the dark
        bedroom
          for sleep to take me away
     Passes with tick
      and tock
        of the wooden clock,
And I hear also
  in my imagination
    The silent breathing
      in   out
        in   out
Of a thousand other
  listeners to the night.
Cats stalk the slates
On firm and soundless feet
And tear the darkness with their yowls.
The joists and timbers
    stretch and sigh,
Ghosts in the attic creak,
    And dew beads the listening sycamore
That inks the space
  between me and the indifferent moon.

And this is the hour, perhaps
That will never be,
That will be looped into time
As the clocks of England
Adjust after their long summer
        To the rigours of Greenwich.

A child turns in its sleep
And somewhere an aged tap
            drips and drips.

GERARD BENSON

A Leaf Treader

I have been treading on leaves all day until I am
    autumn-tired.
God knows all the colour and form of leaves I have
    trodden on and mired.
Perhaps I have put forth too much strength and been too
    fierce from fear.
I have safely trodden underfoot the leaves of another year.

All summer long they were overhead, more lifted up
    than I.
To come to their final place in earth they had to pass
    me by.
All summer long I thought I heard them threatening
    under their breath,
And when they came it seemed with a will to carry me
    with them to death.

They spoke to the fugitive in my heart as if it were leaf
    to leaf.
They tapped at my eyelids and touched my lips with an
    invitation to grief.
But it was no reason I had to go because they had to go.
Now up my knee to keep on top of another year of snow.

ROBERT FROST

October Boy

If you can catch a leaf, so they say
    As it falls from the tree,
        Glad will you be,
    For a year and a day.

But I say let the leaves lie on the ground.
    I will find my delight
        Galloping right
    Into this rustling mound.

Let others snatch happiness from the trees
    I will jump in this deep
        Mouldering heap
    Up to my knobbly knees.

VIRGINIA GRAHAM

I thought it was interesting that Robert Frost in America and Virginia Graham in Britain, were both 'up to their knees' in leaves — though she does admit that hers were 'knobbly'. I didn't know that to catch a falling leaf brought good luck.

I've never grown out of my liking for shiny brown conkers, and hope I never will. In this next poem the fruits from 'a tropical childhood' refer to Grace Nichols' Guyanese childhood.

Conkers

Autumn treasures
from the horsechestnut tree

Lying roly poly
among their split green casings

Shiny and hard
like pops of polished mahogany

An English schoolboy
picking them up —

The same compulsive
fickle avidity —

As I picked up
orange-coloured cockles

Way back then
from a tropical childhood tree

Hand about to close in . . .
then spotting another even better

Now, waiting on our bus
we grown-ups watch him

Not knowing how or why
we've lost our instinct

For gathering
the magic shed of trees

Though in partyful mood
in wineful spirits

We dance around crying,
'Give me back my conker.'

GRACE NICHOLS

Guisers

Up the echo-flights of stair-wells,
Down each dank, gas-mantled close,
Clatter children, dressed in ghost-sheets,
Towels and hats, old-curtain cloaks,
Smocks they haven't cottoned on to . . .

Little guisers, daubed with lip-stick,
Burnt-cork beards, moustaches, rouge —
In their hands or slung from branches
Flicker faces, fiery ghouls;
Scooped-out root-crops, orange gourds.

Nightlights gleam through parchment skin,
(Smell of wax-baked vegetable);
Pots, with heat-crimped lids, ill-fitted,
Empty of what's edible,
Mimic crudely trepanned skulls!

Shrivelled, shrunken heads of Java,
Strung on knotted sisal threads,
Shaven wedge-chins of cadavers,
Exhumed corpses, traitors' heads,
Show what love, half-smiling, dreads —

Each child has a gruesome double!

Rough-cut sockets flare and ogle,
Chunk-teeth, daggered, grin and leer,
Severed night-heads bob and dangle,
Looming out a pagan cheer —
Let the shining Saints appear!

Angel children/evil spirits
Rush, and dawdle, in and out,
Keen to trick you if you will not
Treat them in this season's rout
To the trials — and their reward.

Apples bobbing in a zinc bath,
To be had by bite, not grasp,
Scones too, strung across the kitchen,
Treacle-dripping — laugh and gasp —
'In your mouth now, mind your clothing.'

But the neighbours get their own back
For the welcome and the jests,
All must sing — or do their pieces —
Mischief-makers bless as guests —

Fittingly the rites are done
Before All Hallows frosty sun.

TOM DURHAM

This poem is filled with firelight and shadow and dramatic images. It would speak aloud rather well, as a class Hallowe'en poem. The word 'Guiser' is an old word for actor or mummer; in this case a 'Disguiser'.

November 3rd

A rocket with its stick
jammed into the ground
snatched from the box
when no one was looking

into the garden under my coat
rammed in the earth
when all the backs were turned

Ignition
firing into mud
Stuck fast

Just a couple of sparklers
Mark's Dad had said
as a treat before Guy Fawkes

Now spluttering with rage
    speechless moment then
louder and louder — bellowing

his fury at us
rising higher and higher
'Spoiling everything Everything
Just never enough Never satisfied'

His words like whipping twigs
that sting hot tears
too much shame to hear him
on and on

of how we would have had
some hot tomato soup
and all been happy

not now   No
You two put an end to that
now everyone must do without

Because of us
no treats
no happiness

through all the tears
a blackened twisted wreck
of burned out wood and paper
crushed beneath my boot

MICK GOWAR

Firework Night

The sky is filled with sparks and flames;
the children rush about,
thier cries are hardly heard among
the din of bangers, jumping jacks and rockets.

Dogs howl and cats cry —
Frightened of the noise.
The sky is filled with cordite smoke.
The fire is burning high.
Flashes here and crackles there.
A rocket soars into the sky.

Among all this noise nobody hears
a small child sobbing in the shade,
a banger exploded in his hand
and only he can feel the pain.

ERIC SIMPSON

Homework

I have to write an autumn poem . . .
'Make it rhyme,' she said,
'If you have time.'
I couldn't be worse
At writing verse.
Tomorrow I have to give it in,
So I'll begin.

An autum poem
Needs golden sheaves
And swirling leaves
Of orange, purple, red —
and corn — or bread —
For harvest spread.
Ripe acorns abound;
Shiny conkers hit the ground.
I'd better mention laden trees,
Ripe apples shaken by the breeze . . .
The hedgehog snores,
And diligent squirrel stores,
While swallows leave these shores.
School starts in September:
It's not long till November
With Guy Fawkes to remember.
But spooky Hallowe'en
Comes in between.

Have you written your poem?
Yes, this one's mine. Good. Yes, that's fine.
Now let's do one about Christmas . . .
Oh no! . . . 'pheasant, pleasant, present . . .
Jolly, holly, dolly . . .'

MARGARET PORTER

The Story-book

All Christmas Eve
He passed in a dream
Of scarlet berries,
Prickles gloss-green.
The curtain drawn
He sat at tea
In a paper-rustling
Ecstasy.
He went upstairs
With tinselled string
Tied round. Like a coiled
And tightened spring
On his bed he lay.
Oh, his heart all night
Ran round on shining
Rails of delight!

On New Year's Day
He saw through the pane
Paper and holly
Heaped up to the rain.
And his heart was a draggled
And bonfire thing,
A twisted rail
And a broken spring.
But when dusk had closed
On the mist and damp —

The coal brought in,
And the early lamp
Lighted — oh, then
He turned with a sigh
To the story-book
He had once put by!

JOHN WALSH

True Love

My love was a thousand miles away,
So I rang her up on Christmas Day
(Which cost me more than half my pay).
    So full was my heart
    When I tried to start,
I couldn't think of a word to say.

IAN SERRAILLIER

Christmas Breeze

Auntie would say 'Ah! Christmas breeze',
as the Norther leapt from the continent
across Caribbean seas,
across our hills
to herald Christmas,
ham boiling in the yard
plum pudding in the cloth
(Let three stones bear the pot;
and feed the hat-fanned fire).

This breeze in August cools a Summer's day
here in England
In December in Jamaica
we would have called it *cold*,
Cold Christmas Breeze,
fringing the hill tops with its tumble
of cloud, bringing in
imported apples, and dances
and rum (for older folk).
For us, some needed clothes, and a pair
of shoes squeezing every toe.

And Midnight Mass:
Adeste Fideles!

   Some Faithful came —
and why not? — a little drunk,
some overdressed, but
ever faithful.
Like Christmas breeze

returning every year, bearing
not August's end, nor October's
wind and rain but, Christmas
and 'starlights'
and a certain sadness, except for Midnight Mass
and the Faithful
('The Night when Christ was born').

   I miss celebrations, but I miss most
the people of faith
who greeted warmly every year
the Christmas breeze.

JOHN FIGUERORA

The Pantomime

Regularly at Christmas-time
We're taken to the Pantomime;
We think it's childish, but we go
Because Papa enjoys it so.

GUY BOAS

Waste

Our governess — would you believe
It? — drowned herself on Christmas Eve!
This was a waste, as, anyway,
It would have been a holiday.

HARRY GRAHAM

The Calendar

I knew when Spring was come —
Not by the murmurous hum
   Of bees in the willow-trees,
     Or frills
     Of daffodils,
   Or the scent of the breeze;
But because there were whips and tops
By the jars of lollipops
In the two little village shops.

I knew when Summer breathed —
Not by the flowers that wreathed
   The sedge by the water's edge,
     Or gold
     Of the wold,
   Or white and rose of the hedge;
But because, in a wooden box
In the window at Mrs Mock's
There were white-winged shuttlecocks.

I knew when Autumn came —
Not by the crimson flame
   Of leaves that lapped the eaves
     Or mist
     In amethyst
   And opal-tinted weaves;
But because there were alley-taws
(Punctual as hips and haws)
On the counter as Mrs Shaw's.

I knew when Winter swirled —
Not by the whitened world,
  Or silver skeins in the lanes
    Or frost
    That embossed
  Its patterns on window-panes:
But because there were transfer-sheets
By the bottles of spice and sweets
In the shops in two little streets.

BARBARA EUPHAN TODD

Birthdays

I've separated birthdays from other occasions because there *is* something special about them. Children can hardly wait for the great day. Adults might start groaning about them after about age thirty-five . . . Some of them pretend they are still twenty-one. Others talk about the 'Big FOUR-0' or their 'Half-century'. The position changes in real old age, and 100 is considered an achievement. I couldn't find a poem about being 100 so I've made up this one about a friend's mother, who died just six months after her special day.

Joan, at 100

You were pleased at eleven
when your sculptor father
made a delicate cast
of your left hand

As a young girl, eighteen,
you went camping one Summer
with the poet, Rupert Brooke,
who died in the First World War.

The passing years brought
marriage, three children,
another war, widowhood,
and loss of friends.

Now, aged one hundred
you are surprised to find
your face in the local paper,
a telegram from the Queen.

Candida

for John Betjeman's Daughter

Candida is one today,
What is there that *one* can say?
One is where the race begins
Or the sum that counts our sins;
But the mark time makes tomorrow
Shapes the cross of joy or sorrow.

Candida is one today,
What is there for me to say?
On the day that she was one
There were apples in the sun
And the fields long wet with rain
Crumply in dry winds again.

Candida is one and I
Wish her lots and lots of joy.
She the nursling of September
Like a war she won't remember.
Candida is one today
And there's nothing more to say.

PATRICK KAVANAGH

(Another) Rhymer

I was One
I'd just . . .

I was Two
no longer . . .

Then at Three
I felt like . . .

When I was Four
I'd grown some . . .

At Five
I was fully . . .

Then at Six
I played around with coloured . . .

At Seven
Life was . . .

And at Eight
I found a . . .

When I was Nine
The world was . . .

When I was Ten
we built a . . .

But when I was Eleven
I ran out of rhymes.

MATT SIMPSON

Birthdays

My friend has a birthday;
And what can I say
To young Betty Blake
With her wonderful cake
And seven pink candles there —
One candle for every year?
'How many candles shall I see
On yours?' asked Betty Blake of me.
'Sixty!' I cried, excited by it —
Steady, old heart! Lie quiet!

W H DAVIES

This poem was probably written in the 1920s or 1930s — it has an old-fashioned feel to it, compared to the modern one that follows.

Betty at the Party

'When I was at the party,'
  Said Betty, aged just four,
'A little girl fell off her chair
  Right down upon the floor;
And all the other little girls
  Began to laugh, but me —
I didn't laugh a single bit,'
  Said Betty seriously.

'Why not?' her mother asked her,
  Full of delight to find
That Betty — bless her little heart! —
  Had been so sweetly kind.
'Why didn't you laugh, my darling?
  Or don't you like to tell?'
'I didn't laugh,' said Betty,
  ' 'Cause it was me that fell.'

ANON

The Birthday Cake

O why did Mavis have to make
Me such a soppy birthday cake,
With icing pink and ribbon red?
Why couldn't she have made instead
A cake of which I could be proud —
Aren't FA Cup-shaped ones allowed?

COLIN WEST

Little Brother's Secret

When my birthday was coming
Little Brother had a secret
He kept it for days and days
And just hummed a little tune when I asked him.
But one night it rained
And I woke up and heard him crying.
Then he told me.
'I planted two lumps of sugar in your garden.
Because you love it so frightfully
I thought there would be a whole sugar tree for your
birthday
And now it will all be melted.'
O, the darling!

KATHERINE MANSFIELD

Just in Case

When it's nearly my birthday
And so that people won't be upset
Or forget,
I always think it's kinder,
Just as a reminder,
To leave notes on plates,
Hinting at dates.

MAX FATCHEN

Scouser's Birthday Card

Todaze yer sumpthink berfdee, ma,
   I want yer terrav a gud time,
So to cheer yerrup on y'berfdee, mam,
   I've rit for yer diss pome.

MATT SIMPSON

Scouser is slang for 'someone from Liverpool' — a Liverpudlian. I like the contrast between Matt Simpson's greeting to his ma, and Christina Rossetti's to her mother, nearly a hundred and fifty years earlier. (I share Mrs Rossetti's birthday!)

To My Mother

(Presented with a Nosegay)

Today's your natal day;
   Sweet flowers I bring:
Mother, accept I pray
   My offering.

And may you happy live,
   And long us bless;
Receiving as you give
   Great happiness.

27 April 1842

CHRISTINA ROSSETTI

Grandmamma's Birthday

Dear Grandmamma, with what we give,
We humbly pray that you may live
For many, many happy years:
Although you bore us all to tears.

HILAIRE BELLOC

Marty's Party

Marty's party?
Jamie came. He
seemed to Judy
dreadful rude. He
joggled Davy,
spilled his gravy,
squeezed a melon
seed at Helen,
gave a poke so
Eddy's Coke so
fresh and fizzy
showered Lizzy;
jostled Frank who
dropped a hank
of juicy candy.
Debby handy —
double bubble
gum in trouble —
Debbie mebbie
stumbled, bumbled
into Jessie.
Very messy!
Very sticky!

That's a quickie —
not so ludi-
crous to Judy,
watching Jamie
jilting Amy,
wilting Mamie,
finding Vicky.

What a tricky
lad! Where's Marty?
Don't know. She just
gave the party.

DAVID McCORD

Waiting

Waiting, waiting, waiting
  For the party to begin;
Waiting, waiting, waiting
  For the laughter and din;
Waiting, waiting, waiting
  With hair just so
And clothes trim and tidy
  From top-knot to toe.
The floor is all shiny,
  The lights are ablaze;
There are sweetmeats in plenty
  And cakes beyond praise.
Oh the games and dancing,
  The tricks and the toys,
The music and the madness
  The colour and noise!
Waiting, waiting, waiting
For the first knock on the door —
Was ever such waiting,
  Such waiting before?

JAMES REEVES

Birthday

Beloved dog, in from the wet
Reeking of earth, licking my face like a flame,
Your red-brown coat and glowing eyes
Clearer than anything in human nature
Tell me I will live another year.

JAMES MERRILL

The Barkday Party

For my dog's birthday party
I dressed like a bear.
My friends came as lions
and tigers and wolves and monkeys.
At first, Runabout couldn't believe
the bear was really me. But
he became his old self again
when I fitted on his magician's top hat.
Runabout became the star, running about
jumping up on chairs and tables
barking at every question asked him.
Then, in their ordinary clothes,
my friend Brian and his dad arrived
with their boxer, Skip. And with us
knowing nothing about it, Brian's dad
mixed the dog's party meat and milk
with wine he brought. We started
singing. Runabout started to yelp

All the other six dogs joined —
yelping
> *Happy Barkday to you*
> > *Happy Barkday to you*
> *Happy Barkday Runabout*
> > *Happy Barkday to you!*

JAMES BERRY

Revenge

I hate you, I hate you, I hate you, Anne Scully!
I hope a gorilla traps you in a gully!
Here are some curses I'm putting on you:
Measles at Christmas, at Easter the flu.
That you lose your bus ticket and meet an inspector
Who'll shove you right off with a loud public lecture.
I hope that at ballet, when up on your toes,
You'll look down and find out you're wearing no clothes.
At school, in your lunch-box, instead of a cake,
I hope you'll discover a poisonous snake.
If royalty asks you to supper, you twerp,
I hope you'll spill gravy, and then loudly burp.
And when you go swimming, I hope a fierce creature
With ten-metre molars pops up to eatya!
You want to know why! Just listen then, smarty:
I wasn't invited to your birthday party!

ROBIN KLEIN

Happy Birthday from Bennigans

Why did you do it, Mother?
I told you — didn't I — that I'd go with you
to a restaurant for my birthday
on one condition: Don't go and blab
to the waitress it's my BIG DAY.
But you had to go and tell her.
God, what if somebody had seen me?
I realise that you and Daddy
simply do not care if you ruin my reputation.
I almost thought for a teensy second
you had restrained yourself for once.
But no. You and your big mouth.
'Hip, hop, happy, b, birth, day,
hap, hap, happy, Happy Birthday to You!':
a zero girl, singing a zero song
at the top of her nothingness of a voice.
'All of us at Bennigans hope it's a special day!'
All of them, Mother, not just some.
That's IT for birthdays from now on.
Next year I'll be celebrating by myself.

JULIE O'CALLAGHAN

No School

Today

Three magic words that conjure up time for the outings, sports, holidays, and playtimes in some of these poems. Others tell of more restricted events, like those days when someone smart comes to tea. 'Why have we got the best tea-set out?' I would ask, and then shut up at a warning look from my mother.

Like Bubah and Zaida in Michael Rosen's poem, my grandparents came from other countries. We visited them most Sundays, and I was always sick on the bus journey. Nana recited poems to us, and Papa gave us shillings to take home.

The last poem here, 'Hard Cheese', brings back the fields behind our house where we played for hours with the girls from next door . . . until the inevitable 'Time for Bed!' meant that the freedom was over.

Totteridge Fields

No school tomorrow
So we stayed up later,
Until the sun went down,
Until the familiar field
grew chill and shadowy.

We played at houses quietly;
Loud voices might alert
Parents in both our houses.
The stubbly summer hay
prickled our bare legs.

Our play was close and secret.
We drank pretend tea
Out of home-made cups
Moulded with squidgy clay
from the forbidden brook.

When they called 'Time for bed'
As we knew they would,
We gathered sandals, rug,
Silent, trailed home
through our adjoining gates

Dreaming about tomorrow.

Bubah and Zaida
(Visiting Mum's Mum and Dad)

We sometimes see them on Sunday.
They live in a dark room at the end of a dark corridor
and Bubah kisses us all when we arrive.
She looks like mum but very silver and bent at the
    middle,
which we will all look like one day says Mum's father.
Dad always looks fed up because he doesn't want to come
but Mum talks to them properly.
Zaida looks tired
and pretends that the half crown he's going to give me
disappears into the ceiling along with my nose
if I'm not careful — snap — and there's his thumb in his
    fist,
and he beats me at draughts, dominoes, snap,
    hare-and-hounds,
and even dice
and he's got a bottle with a boat in it
and we go for walks on Hackney Downs
which he calls Acknee Dans.

And all the old men there say, 'Hallo, Frank,'
and while we're walking along he says:
'What's to become of us, Mickie, what's to become of
    us?'
and I don't know what to answer.
And he shows me to Uncle Hymie
who looked out of his window and said:
'Is that big boy your grandson, Frank?' (even though he
    knows my name)
because that's the way they talk.
And when we get back we eat chopped herrings or
    chopped liver
which is my favourite
and Bubah tells stories that go on for hours
about people she knows who are ill or people who've
had to pay too much money and at the end of the story
it always seems as if she's been cheated.
And once she took a whole afternoon to tell Mum
how to make pickled cucumber and she kept saying:
'Just add a little salt to taste, a little salt to taste,
just taste it and see if there's enough salt,
to make sure if there's enough salt — just taste and see.'
And she calls me, 'Tottala,' and rubs my hair and bites
    her lips
as though I'm going to run away
and so she shakes her head and
says, 'Oy yoy yoy yoy yoy.'
But Zaida goes to sleep in the old brown armchair
with his hands on the pockets of his flappy blue trousers
and when we go Mum frowns

and Zaida holds my hand in his puffy old hand,
keeps ducking his head in little jerks
and says to us all, come again soon,
but I'd be afraid to go all the way on my own
and it's very dark and the lavatory is outside
which is sometimes cold.
She doesn't like it when we go,
and she kisses us all over again
and Dad walks up and down like he does at the station
and Mum keeps pushing me and poking me
and they both wave all the time we go away into the
     distance
and I always wave back because I think they like it
but Mum and Dad sit absolutely quiet
and nobody speaks for ages.
Mum says Zaida shouldn't give me the money.

MICHAEL ROSEN

My Mother's People

'When my people come to dinner
Make things tidy,' Mother said.
'Tablecloths and proper napkins;
Hoover underneath the bed.

Proper straight-backed chairs at table,
Doilies underneath the cake,
And make sure that there's a salt-spoon,
Iron the cloth, for goodness' sake.

Shut the dog up while they're eating,
See the knives and forks all glow,
Wash up quickly after dinner,
But not before my People go!'

Dear Mother, I do love your people,
But these people now are mine.
They have come to lunch, not dinner,
Sitting comfy, drinking wine.

Not on straight-backed chairs, but sprawling,
With their plates upon their knees,
Chatting, laughing, having seconds,
While the dog lolls at his ease.

We both love to entertain them,
And maybe my way offends,
But each must find *his* style, *his* fashion,
Then these people are our friends.

DAVID KING

Thomas Hood (1799-1845) wrote many funny poems. How often we'd like to speak the truth (in brackets) while being polite to someone on the surface.

Domestic Asides; or *Truth, in Parentheses*

'I really take it very kind,
This visit, Mrs Skinner!
I have not seen you such an age —
(The wretch has come to dinner!)

'Your daughters, too, what loves of girls —
What heads for painters' easels!
Come here and kiss the infant, dears, —
(And give it, p'rhaps the measles!)

'Your charming boys I see are home
From Reverend Mr Russells;
'Twas very kind to bring them both, —
(What boots for my new Brussels!)

'What! Little Clara left at home?
Well, now, I call that shabby:
I should have loved to kiss her so, —
(A flabby, dabby babby!)

'And Mr S, I hope he's well;
Ah! though he lives so handy
He never now drops in to sup, —
(The better for our brandy!)

'Come, take a seat — I long to hear
About Matilda's marriage;
You're come, of course, to spend the day!
(Thank Heaven! I hear the carriage!)

'What! Must you go? Next time I hope
You'll give me longer measure;
Nay — I shall see you down the stairs —
(With most uncommon pleasure!)

Goodbye, Goodbye! remember all,
Next time you'll take your dinners!
(Now, David, mind I'm not at home
In future to the Skinners!)

THOMAS HOOD

Tomorrow's the fair
And I shall be there
Stuffing my guts
With ginger nuts.

ANON

Hamnavoe Market

No school today! We drove in our gig to the town.
Daddo bought us each a coloured balloon.
Mine was yellow, it hung high as the moon.
A cheapjack urged. Swingboats went up and down.

Coconuts, ice-cream, apples, ginger beer,
Routed the five bright shillings in my pocket.
I won a bird-on-a-stick and a diamond locket.
The Blind Fiddler, the broken-nosed boxers were there.

The booths huddled like mushrooms along the pier.
I ogled a goldfish in its crystal cell.
Round every reeling corner came a drunk.

The sun whirled a golden hoof. It lingered. It fell
On a nest of flares. I yawned. Old Madge our mare
Homed through a night black as a bottle of ink.

GEORGE MACKAY BROWN

The Race

They were never real eggs. The sun
was hotter then, round on a bright blue sky
like the way I painted it. My knees
wore different scabs all summer.

The winner stood on a beer crate, smirking,
whilst the others sulked. One year, I had a plan
and stole a fresh egg from our kitchen.
It was lighter, sat in the deep spoon safely.

Childhood is running forever for a faraway tape,
I was always last, but that day
sped away from the others, a running commentary
coming from nowhere in my head.

I was still in front when the egg fell,
leaving only sunlight in my spoon. I turned
as Junior 4 rushed past, ran back
and knelt to scoop the yolk up from the grass.

CAROL ANN DUFFY

High Dive

Intent, withdrawn, the child-face now severe,
Mind mastering each muscle, first she stands
Upon a pinnacle of loneliness; mustering strength,
Crystallizing purpose, solitary against summer's sky.
For a moment waits there while the voice of fear
Loosens her limbs, cajoling in her ear;
Then, resolute at length,
Taut, tense, with arrowing hands
Curves in a hawk-plunge, sun-doomed-Icarus hurled;
The blade that is her body slicing sheer
The water's haven, secret, sheltering.
And now the crowd applauds her with a sigh —
Rapt, without word
For flight without the succour of a wing.

Today she has known the heart-beat of a bird
And learnt, today, the rhythm of a world.

MARGARET RHODES

*In Greek mythology, Icarus flew with his father Daedalus from Crete,
but the sun melted the wax that held his wings on and he swooped down
to the sea.*

Skating

When I try to skate,
My feet are so wary
They grit and grate;
And then I watch Mary
Easily gliding,
Like an ice-fairy;
Skimming and curving,
Out and in,
With a turn of her head,
And a twirl and a spin;
Sailing under
The breathless hush
Of the willows, and back
To the frozen rush;
Out to the island
And round the edge,
Skirting the rim
Of the crackling sedge,
Swerving close
To the poplar root,
And round the lake
On a single foot,
With a three, and an eight,
And a loop and a ring;
Where Mary glides,
The lake will sing!
Out in the mist
I hear her now
Under the frost
Of the willow-bough

Easily sailing,
Light and fleet
With the song of the lake
beneath her feet.

HERBERT ASQUITH

Winter Sports

The ice upon our pond's so thin
That poor Mama has fallen in!
We cannot reach her from the shore
Until the surface freezes more.
Ah me, my heart grows weary waiting —
Besides, I want to have some skating.

HARRY GRAHAM

The Skateboard

My daddy has bought me a skateboard;
   He tried it out first at the store.
And that is the reason why mommy
   says daddy can't walk anymore.

WILLARD ESPY

Going down Hill on a Bicycle

A Boy's Song

With lifted feet, hands still,
I am poised, and down the hill
Dart, with heedful mind;
The air goes by in a wind.

Swifter and yet more swift,
Till the heart with a mighty lift
Makes the lungs laugh, the throat cry: —
'O bird, see; see, bird, I fly.

'Is this, is this your joy?
O bird, then I, though a boy,
For a golden moment share
Your feathery life in air!'

Say, heart, is there aught like this
In a world that is full of bliss?
'Tis more than skating, bound
Steel-shod to the level ground.

Speed slackens now, I float
Awhile in my airy boat;
Till, when the wheels scarce crawl,
My feet to the treadles fall.

Alas, that the longest hill
Must end in a vale; but still,
Who climbs with toil, wheresoe'er,
Shall find wings waiting there.

HENRY CHARLES BEECHING

*This is an old poem, probably written in the early part of this century. I
often say lines to myself (or out loud) when I feel that sort of freedom on
my bicycle.*

Kevin Scores!

Kevin flicks the ball sideways, leaning
From it, letting it roll
Away, smoothly. He knows Tom is sprinting
Up from defence for it, down
The touchline, so he moves seriously beyond
The centre-half, hoping the ball will come
Over, perfectly, within the reach
Of his timed leap, so he can dive upward,
Feet pointed, arms balancing,
Arched like a hawk for the stab of his head at the goal.

He has seen it often, Law
And Osgood on the telly,
How they wait hungrily
Under the ball floating over,
Then the great poise of the leap,
Almost too late you'd think,
Like great cats hunting,
Or sleek, muscular sharks,
Leaping beyond gravity, up, up,
Then the sharp snap of the head
And the white ball coldly in the net.

Kevin waits by the far post, willing
Tom to get the ball over.
He feels slack and alone, he can see
David in goal, elbows tensely bent, fingers
Stretched for catching in his old woollen gloves.
Tom sways inside the back, he takes
Two short steps, he swings

His left foot, and the ball lifts
Perfectly, perfectly,
Within the bound of Kevin's timed leap.
He is drawn to it, he straightens
In a slow upward dive, and he bends back,
Eyes rapt on the crossed ball he rises
To meet, and now
The sharp snap of his head
And the white ball coldly past the plunging David.

As he runs downfield he knows his face is laughing.

LESLIE NORRIS

From a New Boy

When first I played I nearly died.
   The bitter memory still rankles —
They formed a scrum with *me* inside!
   Some kicked the ball and some my ankles.
I did not like the game at all,
   Yet, after all the harm they'd done me,
Whenever I came near the ball
   They knocked me down and stood upon me.

RUPERT BROOKE

Lord Neptune

Build me a castle,
the young boy cried,
as he tapped his father's knee.
But make it tall
and make it wide,
with a king's throne just for me.

An echo drifted on the wind,
sang deep and wild and free:
Oh you can be king of the castle,
but I am lord of the sea.

Give me your spade,
the father cried;
let's see what we can do!
We'll make it wide
So it holds the tide,
with a fine throne just for you.

He dug deep down
in the firm damp sand,
for the tide was falling fast.
The moat was deep,
the ramparts high,
and the turrets tall and vast.

Now I am king,
the young boy cried,
and this is my golden throne!
I rule the sands,
I rule the seas;
I'm lord of all lands, alone!

The sand-king ruled
from his golden court
and it seemed the wind had died;
but at dusk his throne
sank gently down
in Neptune's rolling tide.

And an echo rose upon the wind,
sang deep and wild and free:
Oh you may be king of the castle,
but I am lord of the sea.

JUDITH NICHOLLS

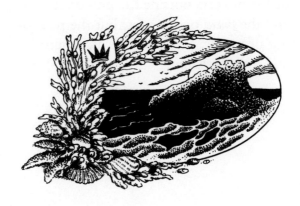

Daft Davy at the seaside

(i)

The new day
Flooded the green bay
In a slow explosion of blue
Sky and silver sand and shimmering sea.
Boots in hand, he paddled the brilliancy
Of rippled wavelets that withdrew,
Sucking his splay grey
Feet in play.

(ii)

It was magic — the brightness of air,
the green bay and wide arc of the sea,
with the rock-pools reflecting his stare
and a maze of wind-sculpted sand-dunes where
slum streets and the Quayside should be.

It was music — not only the sound
of the buskers outside the pub door
and the band on the pier, but the pound-
ing of waves, the loud kids all around,
and gulls screaming shrill on the shore.

It was magic and music and motion —
there were yachts sweeping smooth in the bay
and black steamers white-plumed in mid-ocean;
and ice-cream, candy floss and commotion
as the Switchback got under way.

RAYMOND WILSON

I do like to be beside the seaside,
I do like to be beside the sea,
I do like to stroll upon the Prom, Prom, Prom,
Where the brass bands play
Tiddely om pom pom!
So just let me be beside the seaside
I'll be beside myself with glee,
And there's lots of girls beside
I should like to be beside,
Beside the seaside,
Beside the sea!

JOHN A GLOVER-KIND

My grandfather was a Music Hall singer and comedian and used to sing
this to us.

Summer Afternoon

Mr Punch, slapstick and swagger,
Clobbers the guts out of the afternoon:

In a clatter of chatter
Up comes Judy — that's one!
Up comes the doctor — that's two!
Up comes the policeman — that's three!
With a wallop round the chops
And a squeaky-voiced boast —
'That's the way to do it!'

Stealthily,
Up comes the yawning-jawed crocodile,
Sniffing sausages,
And up dances, Joey, grinning to give the game away

All in play, kids (and dads) crane forward till

A welter of wisecracks
Helter-skelter
Over puppets, showman, kids and dads —
And it's all over.

NEXT SHOW: FOUR TWENTY
Till when — the afternoon's empty

ROBERT LEACH

Farewell to the Farm

The coach is at the door at last;
The eager children, mounting fast
And kissing hands, in chorus sing:
Good-bye, good-bye, to everything!

To house and garden, field and lawn,
The meadow-gates we swang upon,
To pump and stable, tree and swing,
Good-bye, good-bye, to everything!

And fare you well for evermore,
O ladder at the hayloft door,
O hayloft where the cobwebs cling,
Good-bye, good-bye, to everything!

Crack goes the whip, and off we go;
The trees and houses smaller grow;
Last, round the woody turn we swing:
Good-bye, good-bye, to everything!

ROBERT LOUIS STEVENSON

Milking

When I was small, the Irish summers meant cows.

Their flanks reared up colossal in my squint-eyed toddler
   view,
Friesian White and glossy, hairy black,
Spotted with currant-like flies,
And, perched on knobbly-kneed legs, their sides
Heaving placidly as their jaws ripped apart the earth,
Sucking the dewy grass from its brown grasp.
Tagged ears glittered in the sun, and the thundery day
   was smooth and silent
Except for the grass screaming, and the clouds gasping in
   the sky.

Then evening slowly crept over the field,
Dragging its dark cloak over the sky,
Bringing the storm.
Lightning crackled brilliantly, nightmare Christmas tree
   lights
Thunder was like the roar of an enraged beast
Filling my ears with a hissing rush of rain,
Icy, plump drops spattering the grass, more liberal than
   the dew.

The cows were in the milking shed, and I ran in to
   them —
Watched the silver spiders on their udders, sucking the
   live milk
Away — seething white like their haunches, I
Smelt feed in the bins in the hay-barn, felt

Comforting warmth of cow near me.
An electric lullaby soothed me,
Drowning out the lightning and harmonising with the
    thunder.
A cow near me blinked and waggled her long eyelashes
    at me.
I craned to see her ear-tag. She was called C17.

AVRIL HUSTON

Going on the Sunday School Outing

Duffle bag packed and a shilling to spend because I'm
going on the Sunday School Outing
my sandwiches are egg, but I wanted stuffed pork roll
going on the Sunday School Outing
and it's off to the Wirral, that's miles away from here
going on the Sunday School Outing
through the Tunnel we go, on a double-decker bus
going on the Sunday School Outing
and I can sing upstairs though I don't know the words
going on the Sunday School Outing
tunes like The Quartermaster's Stores, and Ten Green
    Bottles
going on the Sunday School Outing
we'll see the river Dee, and then have our mini-rolls
going on the Sunday School Outing

we'll race and fight like pack dogs, whilst the girls play
  rounders
going on the Sunday School Outing
we know no dirty jokes, but we will in twelve months'
  time
going on the Sunday School Outing
who needs religion, when I'm as happy as this through
going on the Sunday School Outing?
it's half past eight at night, as we ride through Bebington
coming from the Sunday School Outing
and the sun's crash-landed just behind Birkenhead
returning from the Sunday School Outing
my arms are all sunburnt, but I've still got the shilling
coming from the Sunday School Outing
that means tomorrow I can buy a Superman comic
I've been on the Sunday School Outing
and I'll relive it all as I try to stay awake
after the Sunday School Outing
I lost my mug on the Sunday School Outing
and my mac on the Sunday School Outing:
I can't wait for the Sunday School Outing

STEWART HENDERSON

Just When . . .

It's always the same.
Just when you're playing a game;
Just when it's exciting
And interesting
With everyone racing
And chasing,
Just when you're having so much fun,
Somebody always wants something done.

MAX FATCHEN

Hard Cheese

The grown-ups are all safe,
Tucked up inside,
Where they belong.

They doze into the telly,
Bustle through the washing-up,
Snore into the fire,
Rustle through the paper.

They're all there,
Out of harm's way.

Now it's *our* street:
All the back-yards,
All the gardens,
All the shadows,

107

All the dark corners,
All the privet-hedges,
All the lamp-posts,
All the door-ways.

Here is an important announcement:
The army of occupation
Is confined to barracks.
Hooray.

We're the natives.
We creep out at night,
Play everywhere,
Swing on *all* the lamp-posts,
Split your gizzard?

Then, about nine o'clock,
They send out search-parties.
We can hear them coming.
And we crouch
In the garden-sheds,
Behind the dust-bins,
Up the alley-ways,
Inside the dust-bins,
Or stand stock-still,
And pull ourselves in,
As thin as a pin,
Behind the lamp-posts.

And they stand still,
And peer into the dark,
They take a deep breath —
You can hear it for miles —
And, then, they bawl,
They shout, they caterwaul:
'J-i-i-i-i-i-mmeeee!'
'Timeforbed. Do'youhearme?'
'M-a-a-a-a-a-reeee!'
'J-o-o-o-o-o-hnneeee!'
'S-a-a-a-a-a-mmeeee!'
'Mary!' 'Jimmy!'
'Johnny!' 'Sammy!'
Like cats. With very big mouths.

Then we give ourselves up,
Prisoners-of-war.
Till tomorrow night.

But just you wait.
One of these nights
We'll hold out,
We'll lie doggo,
And wait, and wait,
Till they just give up
And mumble
And go to bed.
You just wait.
They'll see!

JUSTIN ST JOHN

Game's End

On autumn evenings the children still play in the park,
Scuffing up the sweet-smelling aftermath,
Their shadows in the sunset triple length,
Making heroic kicks, half-legendary saves:
They play until it is dark,
And still for a little while after can be seen
By the flitting of their plimsolls, by their sleeves,
And by the twinkling orb of grass-stained polythene
Rising up white against dark sky or leaves.

Till, by some common consent, the game must close.
No one bothers any more to yell 'Pass' or 'Shoot',
Someone gives the ball a last terrific boot
Into the air and before it falls they are gone,
Wheeling away over the grass,
Snatching their sweaters up from the goalposts, going
Who knows where, only later to see how soon
The white ball never fell, but went on climbing
Into the dark air, and became the moon.

DAVID SUTTON

Forget Not

This

Day

First occasions are very important in our lives, so I was really pleased when I found Zoë Gardner's poem 'Firsts' to open this section. That was a piece of Editor's Luck.

Among the Firsts I remember in my life are:

1) The first time I could ride my bike without falling off.
2) The first time I realised I could read.
3) The first time I went on stage, aged four, in the dancing class show. I wore lipstick, and was scared to close my mouth.
4) The day my first child was born.

There are too many more to mention.

One of the first poems I ever learned as a very small child was from Robert Louis Stevenson's *A Child's Garden of Verses*. It gives a picture of a boy's first experience of the sea.

> When I was down beside the sea,
> A wooden spade they gave to me
>   To dig the sandy shore.
>
> My holes were empty like a cup
> In every hole the sea came up,
>   Till it could come no more —

Firsts

First tinkling laugh,
First wailing cry,
First nagging doubt,
First shameful lie.

First day of school,
First tiny tooth,
First pangs of guilt,
First painful truth.

First white winter morning,
First fresh apple bite,
First star in the sky
On a cool, clear night.

First independence,
First leaving Mum,
First memories,
Firsts still to come.

ZOË GARDNER

from *Tribe*

for Andrea

I was born
on your fourth birthday,
song of the morning dove
spilling from the guava tree.

Grandparents came to look at me,
the number–two girl
with dumpling cheeks and tofu skin.
They pinched and cuddled,
affectionately gruff, blowing garlic breath
across my unflinching face.
Lifting me into their brown speckled arms,
you stood guard, proud and protective
of this new fat sister, stern
like a little Buddha.

I rolled and rebounded,
gravity nestling its fist
in the centre of my stubborn belly,
whereas you were lithe
with the speed of a rabbit,
quick and cunning.
You hopped to errands,
fetching this and that.

We shared papaya boats
Mother emptied of tiny black seeds
that resembled caviar

and eggshells Father hollowed for whistles.
Our lungs expanded
as though they were balloonfish
fluttering out noiseless tunes.
We blew our songs to the gulch
that brought the eucalyptus smell of rain.

I don't remember
going into the forest,
although you must have taken me
where the lilikoi vines
dripped sticky sap passionately,
their blossoms curling like bells or tongues.
I heard my first story from you.

CATHY SONG

from *Louisa, Louisa*

My family is having dinner with the Blairs.
I come early.
Emily shows off her sister Louisa.
Louisa, being only six weeks old, is not interested.
She keeps falling asleep.

'Smile, Louisa,' Emily orders, joggling her.
'Smile for Kate.'
Louisa yawns,
Waves one fist haphazardly and firmly closes both eyes.

'Emily, come and help me put the leaf in the table,'
    Mrs Blair calls.
'Drat!' says Emily. She hands over the baby.
'Hold her,' she commands, and disappears.

So I hold you, Louisa.
I sit very still and
I hold you and watch you sleep
For a moment, you are all mine.
Not that there is much of you . . .
But your eyelids flutter . . . I can feel you breathing . . .
You are terribly alive, Louisa.
There is so much you do not know.
Louisa, you do not know about school!
Do you know words yet, Louisa? No, no words.
You have never heard of dying, Louisa.

. . . Shhh . . . sleep . . .

Louisa, shh.
I love you right now, Louisa, before you know anything,
Before you even know that you are Louisa.

JEAN LITTLE

Where Did the Baby Go?

I cannot remember —
And neither can my Mother —
Just when it was our baby
Turned into my brother.

JULIE HOLDER

from *Ecce Homo*

Suddenly, in the middle of the floor,
Without holding on to anything,
There you are, standing up!
Startled, we all cheer and clap round you: 'clever!'

You stare at us as if we were mad,
Gingerly bend your knees, then brace them:
Just my natural human posture, your face says.
But then you catch on, and clap your hands too,
Sit down with a bump, too hard, and cry a little.

So, you make the great transition:
You are an upright man.
Just for a moment this time:
Soon it will seem primitive to you to crawl.

Imagine the tall noisy individuals you call 'Man!'
Going on all fours down the street!
Such nonchalant pride to join us,
You with your pale hair and face clear as an angel's.
Bare puppy buttocks quivering with pride!

We'll try not to let you down.

DAVID HOLBROOK

Humpty Dumpty Had a Great Fall . . .

What happened to the sand-pits,
        Plasticene models,
        Splash paintings,
And music on Friday afternoons?

What happened to the tooth fairy,
        Father Christmas,
        The Easter bunny,
And fairy tales on Friday afternoons?

What happened to jumping in puddles,
        Walks in the park,
        Trips to the country,
And picnics on Friday afternoons?

Nothing's happened to the sand-pits,
        To the tooth fairy,
        To jumping in puddles,
We just grew a little older on Friday afternoons.

LOUISE FELL

Louise wrote this when she was fourteen and won a prize in a writing competition. It's got rather a sad feel to it — but all the happy occasions are there to remember.

I found you have to experiment with reading this aloud, trying to capture the rhythm and vocabulary of the East Midlands dialect. 'Metab' (last word) is 'my hand'!

First Day at School

it wurorribul m'fost
day at school
memate jeff flewit
went wime
an teacha wunt lerrus
sit next tureachother

went shiwent aht
cockut class cumup
t'me
ansed, 'AH canfaityo
cahnt ah?'
an ah sed eecudnt
an ee sed ee cud
an ah sed ee cuddunt
an eeit me
so ah itim back just
as teacha cumin

shipicked up that
stick as y'point
at bord'we
an crackt m'ovver
edweeit
an sed, 'Widontav
ooligunsere.'

so ah went omm at
playtime an towd
memam
an meman took meback
t'school agen
owdin metab.

BARRY HEATH

Good reader

My little brother's reading really well.
He brings his words home in a little tin
and he can pick out *aeroplane*
from *Pat* and *Peter, dog* and *Jane*.

Oh yes, my brother's reading really well.
He named his rabbits John and Janet,
then Dick and Dora. Now they're Nip and Fluff.
He tries to keep with up the latest stuff.

His teacher says he's reading really well.
He knows this string of words by heart: tree   little
milk   egg   book   school   sit   frog . . . He scores the
  best
marks in his class on every reading test.

It's plain to see he's reading really well.
Yesterday he stopped the talk at breakfast
by asking, *can the rat pat the fat cat?*
My Dad didn't know what to make of that.

He said he'd cancel all my brother's comics,
but Mum said it was all the fault of *phonics*.
He'd soon be back to normal and besides
the clever lad was reading really well.

Ask him what he's reading and immediately
he'll tell you he's on Level 4, Book 3 —
same as last month. He must like that book a lot.
I'm glad my brother's reading really well.

Our Grandma thought that he might like a book
at Christmas, but she had the sense to look
into his room and found one there already.
Oh yes, she said, *he's reading really well.*

She bought him an electric train instead
and now his book is opened up — not read.
It makes a lovely tunnel for the train.
It's lucky that he's reading really well.

BARRY WADE

Anonymous

I know a poem of six lines that no one knows
who wrote, except
                    that the poet was Chinese and lived
centuries before the birth of
Christ. I said it aloud
                once to some children, and when I reached
the last line suddenly they
understood and together all went —
                                    'Ooo!'
imagine that poem, written
                        by a poet truly
who is Anonymous, since
                            in the strict corporeal sense
he hasn't existed for thousands of years — imagine his
                                        little poem travelling
without gas or even a single grease job
across centuries of space and a million
miles of time
            to me, who spoke it
softly aloud to a group of children who heard
and suddenly all together
                        cried 'Ooo!'

MARTIN STEINGESSER

Night Herons

It was after a day's rain:
the street facing the west
was lit with growing yellow;
the black road gleamed.

First one child looked and saw
and told another.
Face after face, the windows
flowered with eyes.

It was like a long fuse lighted,
the news travelling.
No one called out loudly;
everyone said 'Hush'.

The light deepened; the wet road
answered in daffodil colours,
and down its centre
walked the two tall herons.

Stranger than wild birds, even,
what happened on those faces:
suddenly believing in something,
they smiled and opened.

Children thought of fountains,
circuses, swans feeding:
women remembered words
spoken when they were young.

Everyone said 'Hush';
no one spoke loudly;
but suddenly the herons
rose and were gone. The light faded.

JUDITH WRIGHT

New Leaf

Today is the first day of my new book.
I've written the date
and underlined it
in red felt-tip
with a ruler.
I'm going to be different
with this book.

With this book
I'm going to be good.
With this book
I'm always going to do the date like that
dead neat
with a ruler
just like Christine Robinson.

With this book
I'll be as clever as Graham Holden,
get all my sums right, be as
neat as Mark Veitch;
I'll keep my pens and pencils
in a pencil case
and never have to borrow again.

With this book
I'm going to work hard,
not talk, be different —
with this book,
not yell out, mess about,
be silly —
with this book.

With this book
I'll be grown-up, sensible,
and everyone will want me;
I'll be picked out first
like Iain Cartwright:
no one will ever laugh at me again.
Everything will be
different

with this book . . .

MICK GOWAR

I know that feeling so well — new exercise books are almost my favourite thing in life.

Cobweb Morning

On a Monday morning
We do spellings and Maths.
And silent reading.

But on the Monday
After the frost
We went straight outside.

Cobwebs hung in the cold air,
Everywhere.
All around the playground,
They clothed the trees,
Dressed every bush
in veils of fine white lace.

Each web,
A wheel of patient spinning.
Each spider,
Hidden,
Waiting.

Inside,
We worked all morning
To capture the outside.

Now
In our patterns and poems
We remember
The cobweb morning.

JUNE CREBBIN

Nobody at the Window

School's done.
It's 'See you tomorrow, Goodbye!' to the others,
And then off home.
Some of them wait behind to be fetched by their mothers,
But mine is at home.
At the end of the long cold street
Grey with the coming of dusk and a splatter of sleet
In a town turning dark at the edges,
There's tea,
And light and the warmth of a fire,
And the family waiting for me
To tell them all that I've done since I went away
(This morning ever so long ago)
— And the dark shut out.

I give a shout,
And run through the slithering wind
And the speckles of sleet —
Past the lamp-post, the door in the wall, the hedge,
And home.

What's happened?
The gate swings wide.
No one at the window to wave —
Is no one inside?
Nobody in the garden,
Nobody at the door —
Don't we even live here any more?
They didn't say they'd be out.
But the front room's as dark as the street,
Uncurtained and cold.

I run up the empty path with a stitch in my side.
Oh there! At the side of the house a streak of gold,
And the back room curtained,
Aglow.
I remember now . . .
They said they'd be there tonight.
What a silly I've been.
Everything's right after all.
Everyone's in.

MARGARET GREAVES

First Fox

A big fox stands in the spring grass,
Glossy in the sun, chestnut bright,
Plumb centre of the open meadow, a leaf
From a picturebook.

Forepaws delicately nervous,
Thick brush on the grass
He rakes the air for the scent
Of the train rushing by.

My first fox,
Wiped from my eye,
In a moment of train-time.

PAMELA GILLILAN

First Snow

Whose is this long, unexpected elbow
Resting its white sleeve on the wall?
Is anyone out there when I call
To hear my voice? I've lost my echo.

Whose are these feathery tears that keep coming?
Somebody weeps without a sound
And leaves his grief heaped up on the ground.
It's so quiet my ears are drumming.

Whose is that handkerchief on the gatepost
Large enough for a giant sneeze?
Bless you whisper the shivering trees
While I just stand here like a ghost.

Who am I? And where have I woken?
It wasn't the same when I went to bed.
I still feel me inside my head
Though now a different language is spoken.

Suddenly all the meanings have gone.
Is someone trying to tell me something?
A bird shakes silver dust from its wing
And the sky goes on and on and on.

JOHN MOLE

How to Eat a Strawberry

First, sniff —
and then a deep inhale;
note the saliva-flood
round tooth and gum.

Observe seed-studded red,
then feel: Braille promises
through finger-tip and thumb
of tastes to come.

Next — bite;
sink deep incisors
into silken flesh —
let juices run!

Close lips;
grasp, roll the prize
through darkened cave
with curling tongue.

Now — *crush*!
Squeeze, savour, pause;
let juice and pulp invade each cell
with taste of summer sun . . .

until the first fruit's gone.

Now take another one!

JUDITH NICHOLLS

An accident

The playground noise stilled.
A teacher ran to the spot
beneath the climbing frame
where Rawinda lay, motionless.
We crowded around, silent,
gazing at the trickle of blood
oozing its way onto the tarmac.
Red-faced, the teacher shouted,
'Move back . . . get out of the way!'
and carried Rawinda into school,
limbs floppy as a rag doll's,
a red gash on her black face.

Later we heard she was at home,
five stitches in her forehead.
After school that day
Jane and I stopped beside the frame
and stared at the dark stain
shaped like a map of Ireland.
'Doesn't look much like blood,'
muttered Jane. I shrugged,
and remember now how warm it was
that afternoon, the white clouds,
and how sunlight glinted
from the polished bars.

We took Rawinda's 'Get Well' card
to her house. She was in bed,
quiet, propped up on pillows,
a white plaster on her dark skin.

Three days later
she was back at school,
her usual self, laughing,
twirling expertly on the bars,
wearing her plaster with pride,
covering for a week the scar,
she would keep for ever,
memento of a July day at school.

WES MAGEE

*A week after I'd put this poem in the book a little girl called Natalie had
an accident outside my house. The poem kept going through my head as
police, ambulance, mothers and friends — and Natalie — crowded into
my room. Like Rawinda she recovered . . . but with no scar.*

Accidents Happen, But I Wish They Didn't

You can be laughing and joking
one minute, and then
the next, you've caught your finger in the door;
and you can't remember that
there was anything called 'before'.
And all day long
it's 'the day you caught your finger in the door.'

DAVID SCOTT

Weasels

He should have been at school
but instead, he was in bed,
his room more cheerful, brighter,
sheets and pillows whiter
than they'd ever been before.

Comics, bread with crusts cut off,
a jug of homemade lemonade,
Mum's hand so cool against his brow.
Now he had her to himself at last
he'd never want to go to school again.

And all because of little spots,
he raised his vest and thanked them.
Crimson pinpricks on his chest
— some clustered, some quite lonely —
like baby strawberries or beetroot.

Dr Croker joked and felt his muscles.
'Superman! You'll soon be right as rain.'
But his voice from down the stairs
was stern and rather solemn
— and Mummy's sounded scared.

He strained to hear the words,
but they were speaking low. He slipped
out of bed, tiptoed to the door,
pressed his ear against the floor.
'Weasels. He's got weasels, I'm afraid.'

Weasels! He lay in bed and trembled.
Weasels. Furry-grey with pointed teeth.
They must have crept in as he slept,
gnawed and nibbled through the night.
He wondered how much of him was left.

His foot itched. Was it a hidden weasel?
Ankle, knee. Lots of them were there!
He screamed and she came flying.
Her arms were safe as blankets.
He didn't want to stop crying for a while.

JOHN LATHAM

Mumps

I had a feeling in my neck,
And on the sides were two big bumps;
I couldn't swallow anything
At all because I had the mumps.

And Mother tied it with a piece,
and then she tied up Will and John,
And no one else but Dick was left
That didn't have a mump rag on.

He teased at us and laughed at us,
And said, whenever he went by,
'It's vinegar and lemon drops
And pickles!' just to make us cry.

But Tuesday Dick was very sad
And cried because his neck was sore,
And not a one said sour things
To anybody any more.

ELIZABETH MADOX ROBERTS

The boy who gave his writer mother the first line for this poem is called Francis. 'Owen' in line nine refers to the soldier poet Wilfred Owen who died in the first World War.

Asthma Attack

'The flowers in my chest won't open, Mummy,'
The baby voice, like clumsy fingers
Thumbing the harp-strings of your wheeze
Tells me that the air-tight door
Has swung back from the hooks which held it
And slammed on you once more.
Gently I mother and soothe and plug in
Pump and tubes and cover your small face
With a green mask. You look like Owen
Must have when the choking gas
Came down, or like an insect, magnified
With huge mouthpiece and eyes like screens.
You puff the air. I tell you not
To try to talk. The chemicals
With strangely jointed names hiss
Into your lungs. The taut strings
In your accordion chest loosen and sag
And your flowers bloom again.

SUSAN HAMLYN

from *Suzanne at the Hairdresser's*

Robed in white on a lofty throne
I sit before the mirror, alone,

Snip, snip! the scissors clap,
heaping gold upon my lap.

Alone, did I say? there's another me
in the mirror to keep me company

and watch the stray wispy locks
like hours from dandelion clocks

floating down the sunny air.
You'd never think it was my hair!

How hot and still the morning seems,
a day for half-shut eyes and dreams.

Now the mirror rounds a pool;
I peer from out the water cool,

hands and curly head and face —
all is hid below my waist.

What lies below? Perhaps the scales
of a mermaid's twinkling tail.

IAN SERRAILLIER

After the Dentist

My left upper
lip and half

my nose is gone.
I drink my coffee

on the right from
a warped cup

whose left lip dips.
My cigarette's

thick as a finger.
Somebody else's.

I put lip-
stick on a cloth-

stuffed doll's
face that's

surprised when one
side smiles

MAY SWENSON

*This is proof that poets can make poems from anything — even a dental
injection. I know just how she feels (except for the cigarette bit).*

End of a Girl's First Tooth

Once she'd a tooth that wiggled;
Now she's a gap that lisps.
For days she could only suck lollies;
Now she champs peanuts and crithsps.

ROY FULLER

The Sweet-Shop Round The Corner

The child dreaming along a crowded street
Lost hold of his mother, who had turned to greet
Some neighbour, and mistakenly matched his tread
With a strange woman's. 'Buy me sweets,' he said,
Waving his hand, which he found warmly pressed;
So dragged her on, boisterous and self-possessed:
'The sweet-shop's round the corner!' Both went in,
And not for a long while did the child begin
To feel a dread that something had gone wrong:
Were Mother's legs so lean, or her shoes so long,
Or her skirt so patched, or her hair tousled and grey?
Why did she twitter in such a ghostly way?
'O Mother, are you dead?'
                          What else could a child say?

ROBERT GRAVES

Lost in a Shop

From the noisiest end of the crowded store —
Hear that! What a dismal wail!
A little lost girl, stood up on the counter,
As though she were there for sale!

An anxious shop-girl presses her hand;
Her tears fall thickly;
The anxious assistants stare all round . . .
Oh, come someone, and find her quickly!

JOHN WALSH

Getting lost is one of the worst experiences at any age. I still do it.

Goodbye

Goodbye to my blanket
I loved how it stank! It
Was snotty and slimy
And Mum said 'It's time he
Got rid of it, burnt it.'
But I cried 'I want it,
It's cosy, it's snuggly,
Who cares if it's ugly,
It's unique aroma
Reminds me of home. Ah
Blanket, ah blanket,
You're soggy and dank yet
I love every piece of you,
All the smeared grease of you,
All the dried spittle
From when I was little —
It's part of my life now,
We're like husband and wife now!'

Then I met Albert
And now he's my pal, but
He doesn't like gungy
Old blankets all spongy
And sickly and pongy
He says it's all wrong, he
Says I should *blow* up
My blanket, forget it;
To a well-mannered Ted it
Seems utterly nasty,
A part of my past he
Would like to see vanish
So I'm going to be mannish
And grown up and seven,
Send blanket to heaven.
I'm sorry to lose it
But I really must choose. It
Is Albert or blanket
So now I must thank it
(Dear blanket) for keeping —
While waking and sleeping —
Me snug, wipe the tear from my eye
And say 'Blanket, goodbye!'

JOHN MOLE

Quite apart from the clever rhyming of this poem, the subject is close to my heart. I had a cuddly blanket for years and hated giving it up.

Wedding Day

Lillian McEever is bride for the day
Wearing Mummy's old wedding dress long locked away
And a posy of dandelions for her bouquet
And a tiara of daisies.

Birdsong showers silver on Institute Drive
Where Lillian waits for her guests to arrive
And the shouts and the laughter shake the morning alive
There's a wedding today.

Past the brook they wind where the cherry trees bloom
Casting white showers of blossom over bride and groom
And grandmothers dream in curtained front rooms
And remember.

Lillian McEever forget not this day
For Spring mornings die but memories stay
When the past like the dress is long locked away
And the leaves fall.

GARETH OWEN

It was this poem that started the anthology. There's something very imaginative and appealing about it. The rest followed.

Wedding

A ring upon her finger,
  Walks the bride,
With the bridegroom tall and handsome
  At her side.

A veil upon her forehead,
  Walks the bride,
With the bridegroom proud and merry
  At her side.

Fling flowers beneath the footsteps
  Of the bride;
Fling flowers before the bridegroom
  At her side.

CHRISTINA ROSSETTI

Bells

'Ding a ding,'
The sweet bells sing,
And say,
'Come, all be gay,'
For a wedding day.

'Dong a dong,'
The bells sigh long,
And call,
'Weep one, weep all,'
For a funeral.

CHRISTINA ROSSETTI

Grandad

Grandad's dead
And I'm sorry about that.

He'd a huge black overcoat.
He felt proud in it.
You could have hidden
A football crowd in it.
Far too big —
It was a lousy fit
But Grandad didn't
Mind a bit.
He wore it all winter
With a squashed black hat.

Now he's dead
And I'm sorry about that.

He'd got twelve stories.
I'd heard every one of them
Hundreds of times
But that was the fun of them:
You knew what was coming
So you could join in.
He'd got big hands
And brown, grooved skin
And when he laughed
It knocked you flat.

Now he's dead
And I'm sorry about that.

KIT WRIGHT

At The End

The day my great-aunt Sarah died, how I remember well,
She lay alone with daffodils and never rang her bell.
She lay as quiet as her chair and books upon her shelf.
She gave no trouble to her nurse, no trouble to herself.
She was more quiet than the bare, ploughed fields that
    lay outside.
The knowledge in her listening face as certain was,
    and wide.

FRANCES CORNFORD

The Funeral

I was too young
for the funeral,
just six,
sitting plumply
on Grandmother's lawn
that Spring afternoon.
I gathered dewed daisies
and buttercups,
dotted amongst the clover,
threaded their thin stalks
to make a chain.

High afternoon,
I cartwheeled on damp grass
with childish ineptitude.
A dog barked distantly.
On the shaded verandah
my dreamy brother sang wordlessly
as he rolled toy cars
on collision courses to the
flower beds.
I wore my flowered summer dress.

Grandfather's roses
twined round the broken lattice.
Thorny Peace,
and peach-tinted Tea:
full-blown and blowsy.
On the dark mantelpiece
stood photographs of him
looking serious and youthful.
Faded portraits
of a grandfather I hardly knew.

Nameless relations
crowded in for tea,
back from the funeral,
dressed in black.
They smiled at us
and pressed cold, silver coins
into our grubby palms.
We lost them later,
playing among tall hollyhocks
and marguerites.

A slight breeze rose from the sea,
and net curtains billowed
from the open windows.
I caught mysterious whispers
and glimpses of
unknown faces.

We picnicked on thin sandwiches
of pink 'funeral' meats
and salmon.
I set a silver cakestand
on the grass,
not comprehending why
the family was here.

The day was beautiful
for a funeral.

SARAH LUCY DAVIES

Some Days retired from the rest
In soft distinction lie
The Day that a Companion Came
Or was obliged to die.

EMILY DICKINSON

The Poem

Under the trees, Jenny is making daisy chains,
Making a verse.
Her smooth hair falls obliquely beneath her scarlet hat.
'I'm having an inspiration,' Jenny says.
She is ten years old.
She links the daisies, and winds them round her hat.
She links the words, and the poem falls in place.
Later, the threaded flowers will droop and fade.
The threaded words hold promise. They will last.

MURIEL GRAINGER

This was my daughter Charlotte's favourite poem when she was about eight. Karaka trees grow in New Zealand, the writer's birthplace.

When I was a Bird

I climbed up the karaka tree
Into a nest all made of leaves
But soft as feathers.
I made up a song that went on singing all by itself
And hadn't any words, but got sad at the end.
There were daisies in the grass under the tree.
I said just to try them:
'I'll bite off your heads and give them to my little children
    to eat.'
But they didn't believe I was a bird;
They stayed quite open.
The sky was like a blue nest with white feathers
And the sun was the mother bird keeping it warm.
That's what my song said: though it hadn't any words.
Little Brother came up the path, wheeling his barrow.
I made my dress into wings and kept very quiet.
Then when he was quite near I said: 'Sweet, sweet!'
For a moment he looked quite startled;
Then he said: 'Pooh, you're not a bird; I can see
    your legs.'
But the daisies didn't really matter,
And Little Brother didn't really matter;
I felt *just* like a bird.

KATHERINE MANSFIELD

Painting The Gate

I painted the mailbox. That was fun.
I painted it postal blue.
Then I painted the gate.
I painted a spider that got on the gate.
I painted his mate.
I painted the ivy around the gate.
Some stones I painted blue,
and part of the cat as he rubbed by.
I painted my hair. I painted my shoe.
I painted the slats, both front and back,
all their bevelled edges, too.
I painted the numbers on the gate —
I shouldn't have, but it was too late.
I painted the posts, each side and top,
I painted the hinges, the handle, the lock,
several ants and a moth asleep in a crack.
At last I was through.
I'd painted the gate
shut, me out, with both hands dark blue,
as well as my nose, which,
early on, because of a sudden itch,
got painted. But wait!
I had painted the gate.

MAY SWENSON

My Own Day

When I opened my eyes this morning,
The day belonged to me.
The sky was mine and the sun,
And my feet got up dancing.
The marmalade was mine and the squares of sidewalk
And all the birds in the trees.
So I stood and I considered
Stopping the world right there,
Making today go on and on forever.
But I decided not to.
I let the world spin on and I went to school.
I almost did it, but then, I said to myself,
'Who knows what you might be missing tomorrow?'

JEAN LITTLE

Index of First Lines

A big fox stands in the spring grass 129
A ring upon her finger 145
A rocket with its stick 56
A week ago I had a fire 43
All Christmas Eve 60
And is this August weather? Nay, not so 45
Auntie would say 'Ah! Christmas breeze' 62
Autumn treasures 52
Beloved dog, in from the wet 78
Build me a castle 98
Candida is one today 69
Come children, gather round my knee 23
Dear Grandmamma, with what we give 75
Dear March — Come in 30
'Ding a Ding,' 145
Duffle bag packed and a shilling to spend 105
First, sniff 131
First tinkling laugh 113
For my dog's birthday party 78
From the noisiest end of the crowded store 141
Go down to Kew in lilac-time, in lilac-time 40
Good-by my winter suit 33
Goodbye to my blanket 142
'Good morning, my husband,' I said 14
Grandad's dead 146
He should have been at school 134
He was the one man I met up in the woods 24
'I am cherry alive,' the little girl sang 12
I cannot remember— 117
I climbed up the karaka tree 151
I do like to be beside the seaside 101
I had a feeling in my neck 136
I hate you, I hate you, I hate you, Anne Scully! 79
I have been treading on leaves all day 50

I have to write an autumn poem 58
I knew when Spring was come 65
I know a poem of six lines that no one knows 123
I painted the mailbox. That was fun 152
I ran out in the morning, when the air was clean 47
I really take it very kind 87
I sneezed a sneeze into the air 25
I was born 114
I was lying in the bath 35
I was One 70
I was too young 147
If you can catch a leaf, so they say 51
Intent, withdrawn, the child-face now severe 91
It is the first mild day of March 32
It's always the same 107
It was after a day's rain 124
it wurorribul m'fost 120
Kevin flicks the ball sideways, leaning 96
Laden with bud and unfolding leaf 37
Lillian McEever is bride for the day 144
Look at red-faced Winter 28
Look to this day! 11
Marty's party? 76
Mr Punch, slapstick and swagger 102
My daddy has bought me a skateboard 94
My daddy has paid the rent 15
My family is having dinner with the Blairs 116
My friend has a birthday 71
My heart has never beat before 29
My left upper lip 139
My little brother's reading really well 121
My love was a thousand miles away 61
No school today! We drove in our gig to the town 89
No school tomorrow 82

No visitors in January 21
O I have dined on this delicious day 12
O why did Mavis have to make 73
On a Monday morning 127
On autumn evenings the children still play in the park 110
Once she'd a tooth that wiggled 140
Our governess — would you believe 64
Out of his cottage to the sun 31
Regularly at Christmas-time 64
Robed in white on a lofty throne 138
School's done 128
So here we are in April, in showy, blowy April 34
Some days retired from the rest 150
St Agnes' Eve — Ah, bitter chill it was! 25
Suddenly, in the middle of the floor 117
The child dreaming along a crowded street 140
The coach is at the door at last 103
The day my great-aunt Sarah died, how I remember well . 147
The first of April, some do say 35
The flowers in my chest won't open, Mummy 137
The grown-ups are all safe 107
The ice upon our pond's so thin 93
The new day 100
The playground noise stilled 132
The rain stopped for one afternoon 38
The sandy cat by the Farmer's chair 44
The sky is filled with sparks and flames 58
The tread is gone 46
The year's at the Spring 10
They were never real eggs. The sun 90
This day dawning is the black fruitgum 16
This hour in the night 48
Today is the first day of my new book 125
Today's your natal day 75

Tomorrows never seem to stay 18
Tomorrow's the fair 88
Tonight, tonight, the pillow fight 44
Toodaze yer sumpthink berfdee, ma 74
Under the trees, Jenny is making daisy chains 150
Up the echo-flights of stair-wells 54
Waiting, waiting, waiting 77
Way down Geneva 26
We sometimes see them on Sunday 83
What happened to the sand-pits 119
When first I played I nearly died 97
When I opened my eyes this morning 153
When I try to skate 92
When it's nearly my birthday 74
'When I was at the party' 72
When I was down beside the sea 112
When I was small, the Irish summers 104
When my birthday was coming 73
When my people come to dinner 86
Whose is this long, unexpected elbow 130
Why did you do it, Mother? 80
With lifted feet, hands still 94
You can be laughing and joking 133
You know, of course, that pleasant rhyme 42
You were pleased at eleven 68

Acknowledgements

The author and the Publisher would like to thank the following for their kind permission to reprint copyright material in this book:

Random Century Ltd for 'Come Down to Kew' from *Green Fingers* by Reginald Arkell; Anne Bell for 'Greetings' by Anne Bell from *Someone is Flying Balloons* (Omnibus Australia); Catherine Benson for 'Easter Morning'; Gerard Benson for 'Poem for the Changing of the Clocks'; Hamish Hamilton for 'The Barkday Party' by James Berry from *When I Dance* (1988). Reproduced by permission of Hamish Hamilton Ltd. Copyright James Berry; J M Dent and Sons Ltd for 'Goodby, my Winter Suit', by N M Bodecker, from *Hurry, Hurry, Mary Dear;* Macmillan Children's Books for 'Good Times' by Louise Clifton from *Introduction to Poetry,* Part 2, ed. Louis Simpson; Christopher Cornford for 'Autumn Morning at Cambridge' from *Collected Poems,* by Frances Cornford published by Crescent Press (1954) and 'At the End' by Frances Cornford; Kestrel for 'Cobweb Morning' by June Crebbin from *The Jungle Sale.* Reproduced by permission of Penguin Books Ltd; Yale University Press for 'Tribe', and 'Easter, Wahiawa' by Cathy Song Davenport from 'Picture Bride, *Yale Younger Poets Series* (1963); Sarah Davies for 'The Funeral'; Carol Ann Duffy for 'The Race', from *Slipping Glimpses* (The Poetry Book Society 1985); Tom Durham for 'Guisers'; Orchard Books for 'A Day in Spring' by Richard Edwards from *A Mouse in my Ear;* Gervase Farjeon for 'Keep True to Me: A Valentine' by Eleanor Farjeon; Kestrel for 'Just in Case' and 'Just When' by Max Fatchen from *Wry Rhymes for Troublesome Times* (1983). Reproduced by permission of Penguin Books Ltd; Louise Fell for 'Humpty Dumpty had a Great Fall'; Chatto and Windus for 'Christmas Breeze' by John Figuerora from *News from Babylon,* ed. James Berry; Jonathan Cape Ltd and the Estate of Robert Frost for 'A Leaf Treader' from *The Poetry of Robert Frost,* ed. Edward Connery Latham; Roy Fuller for 'End of a Girl's First Tooth' from *The World Through the Window* (1989), published by Blackie Children's Books; Zoe Gardner for 'Firsts'; Pamela Gillilan for 'First Fox' from *Another Second Poetry Book* (Oxford University Press); Collins Publishers for 'November 3rd' by Mick Gowar from *Swings and Roundabouts* (1981); Viking Kestrel for 'New Leaf' by Mick Gowar from *Third Time Lucky* (Viking Kestrel 1988). Reproduced by permission of Penguin Books Ltd; Virginia Graham for 'October Boy'; Muriel Grainger for 'The Poem'; AP Watt Ltd on behalf of The Trustees of the Robert Graves Copyright

Trust for 'Sweetshop Round the Corner' from *Collected Poems* (1975) by Robert Graves; Methuen for 'Nobody at the Window' by Margaret Greaves from *Scrapbox;* Susan Hamlyn for 'Asthma Attack'; Anne Harvey for 'Totteridge Fields' and 'Joan, at 100'; Barry Heath and the John French Agency for 'First Day at School' from *M' Mam Sez*; Hodder & Stoughton for 'Going on the Sunday School Outing' from *A Giant's Scrapbook* (Spire 1989) © Stewart Henderson; André Deutsch Ltd for 'Ecce Homo' by David Holbrook; Julie Holder for 'Where did the baby go?' by Julie Holder from *Another First Poetry Book* compiled by John Foster, published by Oxford University Press; Avril Huston for 'Milking'; The Goldsmith Press Ltd (Newbridge) and Dr Peter Kavanagh (New York) for 'Candida' by Patrick Kavanagh from *Complete Poems;* David King for 'My Mother's People'; Dent Pty/Australia for 'Revenge' by Robin Klein from *Snakes and Ladders* (1985); John Latham for 'Weasles'; Caxton Press for 'Summer Afternoon' by Robert Leach from *Feasts and Seasons;* Oxford University Press for 'My Own Day' © Jean Little 1986. Reprinted from *Hey World, Here I am!* by Jean Little (1986), by permission of Oxford University Press; Harper and Row Inc for 'Louisa, Louisa' by Jean Little from *Hey World, Here I am!;* John Murray (Publishers) and George Mackay Brown for 'A Child's Calendar' from *Fisherman with Ploughs* and 'Hamnavoe Market' from *Voyages* both by George Mackay Brown; Cambridge University Press for 'An Accident' by Wes Magee from *Morning Break;* The Literary Trustees of Walter de la Mare and The Society of Authors as their representative for 'Summer Evening' by Walter de la Mare'; Little Brown and Co USA for 'Marty's Party' by David McCord from *Far and Few* (1983); Harrap Publishing Group Ltd for 'Tomorrows' by David McCord from *Mr Bidery's Spidery Garden* (1972); Atheneum publishers for 'Birthday' by James Merrill; Peterloo Poets for 'First Snow' by John Mole from *The Mad Parrot's Countdown* (Peterloo 1990); Peterloo Poets for 'Goodbye' by John Mole from *Boo to a Goose* (Peterloo 1987); André Deutsch Ltd for 'Good riddance but now what?' by Ogden Nash from *I wouldn't have missed it for the world* (1983); The Virago Press for 'Conkers' by Grace Nichols; Judith Nicholls for 'Lord Neptune' and 'How to eat a Strawberry' © 1990 Judith Nicholls from *Dragonsfire* by Judith Nicholls, published by Faber and Faber and reprinted by permission of the author; Leslie Norris for 'Kevin Scores!' John Murray (Publishers) for 'Kew in Lilac Time' by Alfred Noyes from *Collected Poems;* Orchard Books for 'Happy Birthday from Bennigans' by Julie O'Callaghan from *Taking my Pen for a Walk;* Collins Publishers for 'Wedding Day' by Gareth Owen from *Song of the City;* Margaret Porter for 'Homework';